Ooey-gooey Animals

Sea Anemones

Lola Schaefer

www.raintreepublishers.co.uk

Visit our website to find out more information about **Raintree** books.

To order:

☎ Phone 44 (0) 1865 888112

🖹 Send a fax to 44 (0) 1865 314091

💻 Visit the Raintree Bookshop at www.raintreepublishers.co.uk to browse our catalogue and order online.

First published in Great Britain by Raintree, Halley Court, Jordan Hill, Oxford OX2 8EJ, part of Harcourt Education.
Raintree is a registered trademark of Harcourt Education Ltd.

Editorial: Nick Hunter and Diyan Leake
Design: Sue Emerson (HL-US) and Joanna Sapwell
Picture Research: Amor Montes de Oca (HL-US)
Production: Lorraine Hicks

Originated by Dot Gradations
Printed and bound in China by South China Printing Company

ISBN 1 844 21024 3
07 06 05 04 03
10 9 8 7 6 5 4 3 2 1

British Library Cataloguing in Publication Data
Schaefer, Lola
Sea Anemones
593.6
A full catalogue record for this book is available from the British Library.

Acknowledgements
The publishers would like to thank the following for permission to reproduce photographs: Corbis pp. 4, 5, 9, 13, 16, 22; Eda Rogers p. 21; Graeme Teague p. 12; Jay Ireland & Georgienne E. Bradley/bradleyireland.com pp. 6, 7, 10, 19; Jeff Rotman pp. 1, 15, 17, 18; Minden Picture p. 8 (Fred Bavendam); Photodisc pp. 1, 14; Visuals Unlimited p. 20 (David Wrobel)

Cover photograph of sea anemones, reproduced with permission of Corbis

Every effort has been made to contact copyright holders of any material reproduced in this book. Any omissions will be rectified in subsequent printings if notice is given to the publishers.

CAUTION: Remind children that it is not a good idea to handle wild animals. Children should wash their hands with soap and water after they touch any animal.

Some words are shown in bold, **like this.** You can find them in the glossary on page 23.

Contents

What are sea anemones?

Sea anemones are small animals.

They are soft and have no bones.

Sea anemone bodies are filled with **gel.**

Gel is clear and watery.

Where do sea anemones live?

Sea anemones live in the ocean.

They live on rocks, sand or mud.

Some sea anemones live in cold oceans.

Most sea anemones live in warm oceans.

What do sea anemones look like?

mouth

Sea anemones look like underwater flowers.

Tentacles grow around their mouth.

tentacles

Sea anemones can be many shapes and colours.

This one looks like a strawberry!

What do sea anemones feel like?

Sea anemones feel gooey.

They have **mucus** on their body.

tentacles

It is not safe to touch some sea anemones.

Their **tentacles** can sting.

How big are sea anemones?

Some sea anemones are as small as the tip of your nose.

tentacles

Some sea anemone **tentacles** are thin.

Others are the size of your little finger.

How do sea anemones move?

Sea anemones creep along the ocean floor.

They creep so slowly you might not see them move.

Some sea anemones swim.

Waves can move sea anemones through the water.

What do sea anemones do all day?

Sea anemones rest on rocks or sand.

They wait for food to swim near.

If something bothers them, sea anemones can change shape.

They can look like lumps on a rock.

What do sea anemones eat?

| octopus | tentacles | mouth |

Sea anemones use their **tentacles** to trap or sting small sea animals.

This one is eating a little **octopus**.

tentacles starfish

Sea anemones use their tentacles like fingers.

They push the food into their mouth.

Where do new sea anemones come from?

Most sea anemones make eggs in their bodies.

Later, little sea anemones come out of their mouth.

Some sea anemones do not make eggs.

They pull apart and become two sea anemones.

Quiz

What are these sea anemone parts?

Can you find them in the book?

Look for the answers on page 24.

?   ?

Glossary

gel
thick gooey stuff that some animals have in their body

mucus
slimy stuff that some animals have in or on their body

octopus
sea animal that has eight tentacles

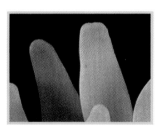

tentacles
long, thin parts that some animals have on their body

Index

Answers to quiz on page 22

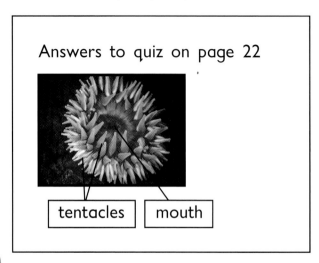

tentacles   mouth

Titles in the Ooey-gooey Animals series include:

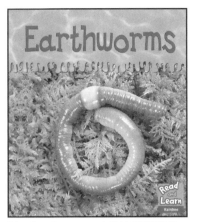

Hardback   1 844 21020 0

Hardback   1 844 21021 9

Hardback   1 844 21022 7

Hardback   1 844 21023 5

Hardback   1 844 21024 3

Hardback   1 844 21025 1

Hardback   1 844 21026 X

Find out about the other titles in this series on our website www.raintreepublishers.co.uk